## Walking Bible Study

# The Path of Justice

Also by Becca Stevens

*Walking Bible Study:*
*The Path of Peace*

*Walking Bible Study:*
*The Path of Love*

*Funeral for a Stranger:*
*Thoughts on Life and Love*

*Hither & Yon:*
*A Travel Guide for the Spiritual Journey*

*Sanctuary:*
*Unexpected Places Where God Found Me*

*Find Your Way Home:*
*Words from the Street, Wisdom from the Heart*
*by the Women of Magdalene*
with an introduction by Becca Stevens

# BECCA STEVENS

Walking Bible Study

# The Path of Justice

ABINGDON PRESS / Nashville

Walking Bible Study
The Path of Justice

*Copyright © 2010 by Abingdon Press*

*This book is printed on acid-free, recycled paper.*

**Library of Congress Cataloging-in-Publication Data**

Stevens, Becca, 1963-
  Walking Bible study / Becca Stevens.
    p. cm.
  ISBN 978-1-4267-1173-2 (v. 2 : alk. paper)
  1. Bible—Devotional literature. 2. Nature—Religious aspects—
Christianity. I. Title.
  BS491.5.S78 2010
  220.071—dc22

                                                              2010022231

10 11 12 13 14 15 16 17 18 19 — 10 9 8 7 6 5 4 3 2 1

MANUFACTURED IN THE UNITED STATES OF AMERICA

*I have been a pastor for sixteen years at*
*St. Augustine's chapel. The congregation has*
*always offered me the freedom to follow my heart*
*and head out to the woods whenever I needed to*
*go. They are even willing to go with me when*
*I need company. This book is dedicated with*
*gratitude to their witness to faith.*

---

*I would like to thank the staff and board of*
*St. Augustine's and Magdalene, who give me*
*work and freedom. A special thanks to Cary*
*Rayson, Tara Armistead, Lisa Froeb, Deb*
*Markland, Susan Sluser, Kay Barry, Donna*
*Grayer, Holli Anglin, Amy Harkness, Jean*
*Hastings, Newell Anderson, Vali Forrister,*
*Peggy McMurray, Mary Murphy, Gladstone*
*Stevens, Kay West, Curtis Shaw, Carlana*
*Harwell, Russ Taff, Allen Karns, Michael Kelsh,*
*Cathy Brown, Jodi Banks, Robin Andrews, and*
*everyone who has shared the trail with me.*

# *Table of Contents*

*The Sacred Ground of Burning Bushes*

# *The Path of Justice*

Welcome to Walking Bible Study, a series of short readings and meditations inviting you into nature and along the many paths to God.

As in life, the walk can be taken alone, with a spouse or friend, or in a group. You can journey up a mountain, into the woods, around the block, or to the flowers in your window box. Wherever you choose to go, remember that the Kingdom is not a place we are headed to, but a place we live in as we walk with God.

In this book we follow the path of justice, considering through Scripture the idea that God is a just God who will hold creation accountable for its behavior. But because his justice is balanced by love and mercy, new creation surrounds us and we have reason to celebrate all the springs in our lives.

# *Using This Book*

Whether you use this book alone, with
a spouse or friend, or in a group, try to set a
pattern that will be intentional and helpful.
Here is one pattern that I have found useful:

Each week:
- Before the walk, read the weekly Scripture and reflection. (If you are walking
  with others, the group may choose to
  read these before gathering.)
- Read Questions for the Walk. These are
  purposely open-ended, to encourage
  thought and discussion during the walk.
- Begin your walk. If you are with a
  group, expect people to fan out along
  the path.
- As you walk, consider the Scripture,
  reflection, and questions; and discuss
  them if you are with others.

- Gather a half-mile before the end of the walk. Listen to the Scripture again.
- Walk the rest of the way in silence.
- At the end of the walk, offer the closing prayer or a prayer of your own.

Each day:
- Read the daily Scripture and meditation.
- Walk if you can.

# *Walking Bible Study*

I have been walking in circles in the woods
of Tennessee for most of my life. This year
I am trying to walk a circle in the woods every
day. I am feeling grateful for every step—rain,
sleet, or shine—and am aware that this is one
of the ways I can pray and commune
with God.

This Bible study is an invitation to walk
more often, with a renewed sense of spiritual
grounding and kinship. It is a call to individuals, couples, friends, and church groups to
leave living rooms and Sunday school classes
and go outside—to the woods, to a park, to
a bench beneath a tree. It is a mindful practice,
like prayer or service.

While we walk, we are leaving no carbon
footprint; we are not eating, drinking, e-mail-
ing, sleeping, or waiting. We are just walking.
Our goal in this study is not to over-think the
Scriptures, not to dress them up for others to

marvel at, but to let them strip us down, to let them form us and sink in like our footprints in the dirt.

Walking in nature is not an afterthought of spiritual development and practice; it is central, historical, and essential. Contemplating the creator of the universe while walking in God's creation opens our hearts and minds to the wondrous gift of life. This walking Bible study can be a kind of field guide, a tool to learn more about Scripture as we travel through the woods and through our lives.

The insights gained while walking will add to the depth and joy of Bible study. A walking Bible study allows us to study Scripture while practicing a spiritual discipline and may provide the permission some need to move from a classroom onto more solid sacred ground. It may be the only way some individuals will feel comfortable opening themselves to Scripture.

Walking is a gentle, neutral activity; it is not intended to stress our bodies, but to focus our energies while our minds wander and empty. Walking can provide the solution to many of life's problems; it is how we make molehills out of mountains. It is how we wander in the desert, find our way on retreat, make our way to altars and through labyrinths.

To those who are not able to walk or who struggle to do it, I want to say that some of my best walks in the woods have included babies in backpacks; friends in wheelchairs; my husband on a cane, able to go just a short distance before the arthritis took hold of him. Accommodating someone who is slow can be a gift; that person is usually miles ahead in other ways.

Trust that the walk is what it needs to be, and trust your fellow walkers. Read the signs offered in front of you, and mark them. Lay aside any worries that are too heavy to carry into the woods, and remember that you can always pick them up when you leave. Carry the minimum: maybe water, pen, paper, a book, a key. You don't need a pack.

Walk—rain or shine, winter or summer—and don't worry.

## Walking in Circles

There is something special about walking in a circle. It is a simple demonstration of the truth that life is a journey, not a destination. It mirrors the world in orbit around the sun and the moon around us. A circle is a symbol of all that is eternal. Our journey begins with God and ends with God; life comes full circle into that truth.

There is a vast difference between walking in a circle and going to a destination. If we have a fixed goal, we can move only in one direction; but our faith journey takes all of us on circuitous routes, sometimes back to the beginning, sometimes around new bends we never expected.

Walking in circles is a way of placing our bodies and minds before the Lord, as did pilgrims, monks, and ascetics before us. Walking on familiar routes frees us up to discover new details and experience different feelings while we walk.

Walking in all weather and during all seasons is an added joy of walking in circles. For twenty years I have walked circles around Radnor Lake, a state park in Tennessee. On a cold, damp winter morning I can tell you where the larkspur, trout lily, and Dutchmen's breeches will bloom come spring. I have felt spiritual renewal like baptism in fresh spring rains. I have felt purified by the cleansing that happens on an August walk at noon, after the sweat, like salty tears, washes away the pain. I have felt awe on a fall afternoon beneath a canopy of leaves that spreads overhead like the ceiling of a cathedral. All these things happen on the same path as I walk the circle again.

## Why We Walk

Walking changes us; it can transport our spirits from being weighed down by life into the joy of God's presence. It can clarify epiphanies, offer us grace, remind us of our need for repentance, and hold us accountable to our brothers and sisters.

Walking is a gift. To go on a spiritual journey without nature as a primary teacher seems like a Eucharist without bread; we miss out on something both symbolic and substantive. Abraham, Buddha, Mohammed, and Jesus all spent defining parts of their ministry in the woods gaining inspiration, insight, rest, and renewal. The woods are our inheritance and offer us a gift. They provide an area for learning and humble us before the creator of the universe.

I have several hopes for this Bible study. I hope that the context in which we study and reflect on the Scriptures will provide new insights into their depth and meaning. I hope that as we become more familiar with the text, we will find the freedom to claim new insights for ourselves, without fear of reprisal or rejection. Finally, I hope that we use this living word to influence the way we walk as we leave the woods and encounter fellow pilgrims in all the places we walk in our lives.

# *Watching the Laundry Dry*

She spent another long afternoon watching
the laundry dry.
The wind blew slow and steady against
Her story hanging out in faded colors.
Frayed shirts talk about how hard it is
To get through rainy seasons.
Patched skirts whisper how easy it is to give up prayers
Never answered anyway.
She could walk up the road that leads north,
But it's lined with a thousand more clotheslines
Draped with similar rags like a Tibetan prayer chain.
Injustice from behind her eyes is clouded
By the foggy memories that rise in silence.
Life is damp and the afternoon drags on.
Still, there is in the depth of her valley,
A small creek that keeps flowing,
So she keeps going down and washing her clothes.

# Week 1. The Prophet's Vision

*Amos 5:14-15, 24, 9:13-16*

## Reflection

We begin with a premise found throughout the history of our faith: that God alone acts upon creation without our interference. The diversity of nature, its order and chaos, its adherence to justice—all these things are unfolding according to the laws of nature and are beyond our control. This premise leads us to humility, admiration, and accountability for our actions.

By studying the laws of nature, we gain insight into the creator of nature. When the prophets observe nature, they see a God who is personal and often unpredictable. But God is also just and will hold creation accountable for its behavior.

Some of the prophets' harshest statements about God involve his dealings with unfaithful servants. Isaiah warns, for example, that God's justice could reduce the earth to its primitive, chaotic state, in which earth and sky would crumble.

God in the Hebrew texts is filled with power that could destroy us, but his justice is balanced by love and mercy. We therefore have reason to be accountable for our actions and try to live more justly.

In this week's reading, Amos calls us to seek good, not evil. Amos was one of the first classic prophets in the Hebrew Scriptures, and he used nature again and again to teach the faithful how to live and serve a just God. If we live justly, says Amos, we may have a chance at life. If we live justly, then the almighty God will treat us justly. If we live justly, we must hate evil, love good, practice fairness in our daily lives, and be open to mercy. It is a great vision, to walk in such a way that all life can thrive.

Amos came from a small town in the Southern Kingdom; he had observed nature firsthand and knew how to read the seasons in the hill country. It is logical that he would speak of God's justice in natural terms and see God's mercy and wrath played out, first and foremost, in the land before him.

It is believed that Amos bred livestock for a living, so his livelihood would have been affected by the severity of a winter or the lack of flowing streams. In Chapter 7, he states that he "was a dresser of sycamore trees," which means he had to cultivate the trees to help make the orchard grow.

Amos preached during a time of prosperity in the eighth century BC. It was also considered a time of religious and social corruption. His message is that because of this corruption, judgment and destruction will be inescapable; we will see it played out in nature.

In the final chapter, though, Amos presents some powerful images of restoration that leave us with a note of hope. He says that the mountains will be dripping sweet wine, and this will be a sign that we have been restored. We can stay, drink the wine, and cultivate our gardens as faithful servants of the Lord.

Today we make huge demands upon the land to feed our own desires for wealth, with little thought about the generations to come. Flying over any city, we see a land that has become a patchwork quilt, cut and stitched to fit our needs. It looks ripped and sewn with our desire to take from it whatever we can. Amos tells us that because of this, someday the earth will tremble.

I offer no judgment of the people who tend the land. I am grateful to them for growing the crops that feed my family. I am grateful to the people who make a living as Amos did, tending animals and trees. But Amos tells us that when justice is carried out, we are going to be held accountable for our actions; and they will cost us.

The prophet's words make me want to love justice and live in greater peace with the land. They make me want to tend my own gardens better and preserve the wildernesses in this world. They make me want to avoid drinking from plastic bottles and buying flowers that are imported. They make me want to do whatever is my part to make justice come.

When Amos says, "Let justice roll down like waters, / and righteousness like an ever-flowing stream" (5:24), I think he means it as both good news and bad news. As good news, the words of Amos urge victims of injustice to "rise up." His words have been used, for example, in the American civil rights movement. Before Martin Luther King, Jr., ever told America about his dream, he stated that African Americans could never be content so long as they could not vote in their own country; that people would never be satisfied until justice rolled down like waters and righteousness like a mighty stream.

The president of the Society of St. Vincent de Paul, whose founder and namesake said in the sixteenth century that there can never be charity without justice, wrote that the faith community around the world is positioned to play a key role as an agent for transformation so that the prophecy of Amos can come true.

As encouraging as these thoughts might be, we can also read Amos' proclamation as bad news. If we are not about advancing the cause of justice in nature and the world, the words of

Amos make it sound as if the waters could rip from us what we thought was ours and leave us destitute. The words describe a day of reckoning and a day to mourn.

The prophet's intention, it seems, is to be faithful to the message he received from God and to deliver it as humbly and honestly as he can. Amos speaks the words out of love for God, as a carrier of God's message, with the hope that we can be the faithful remnant of Joseph.

Amos calls upon nature to make his point to the pre-exilic community. His goal is not to condemn the people for their injustice, but to remind them of God's justice. The words stay with us, not to haunt us or make us feel guilty, but to stir up justice in us again so we carry it into the woods and into a world that needs it so desperately.

## Questions for the Walk

1. Most of us usually don't think of justice in nature. What are your initial thoughts about whether the two are related, and how?

2. What examples in nature do you see of God's love and mercy? of God's judgment?

3. Imagine yourself in the farming or livestock business. How might you view the concept of God's justice in nature?

4. If you, like Amos, had a chance to send a message to the world about nature and justice, what would it be? How would you send it?

*Walk in Silence*

## *Closing Prayer*

Almighty God, in giving us dominion over things on earth, you made us fellow workers in your creation. Grant us wisdom and reverence to use the resources of nature so that no one may suffer from our abuse of them and so that generations yet to come may continue to praise you for your bounty. Bless the lands and waters, and multiply the harvests of the world; let your Spirit go forth, that it may renew the face of the earth; show your loving-kindness, that our land may give her increase; and save us from selfish use of what you give, that men and women everywhere may give you thanks. Increase our reverence before the mystery of life. Give us new insight into your purposes for the human race and new wisdom and determination in making provision for its future in accordance with your will; through Jesus Christ our Lord. Amen.

# Meditations for Week 1

*Day 1*
*Everyone then who hears these words of mine*
*and does them will be like a wise man who*
*built his house on rock. The rain fell, and the*
*floods came, and the winds blew and beat on*
*that house, but it did not fall, because it had*
*been founded on rock. (Matthew 7:24-25)*

When I went walking along a back road near
the woods, I came upon a turtle. He was creep-
ing down the road as if he had all the time in
the world. I followed him for as long as I could
endure walking that slowly.

As we walked, it was impossible not to be
captivated by his curved shell, which looked
like an African sculpture carved in antiquity by
a shaman. The etched shell was made up of a
hundred shades, from black to dark green to
almost pale yellow. It was more intricate than
a labyrinth or a tatted baptismal gown. Maybe

a wiser person, studying the shell, could have read the history of the world on it. I watched the turtle finally make his way to the woods and couldn't help but offer a small genuflection to his wisdom and patience.

I wanted to keep following the turtle but couldn't keep walking at such a slow and steady pace. Maybe lots of us, in our hearts, are more hare than turtle. Yet we want to be the wise person who builds a life on rock, not someone who leaps to faith because it is easy to slip into. We want to be discerning like the turtle, building slowly and digging more deeply than we have before. I am grateful for the turtle's witness.

*Day 2*
*I lift up my eyes to the hills—*
  *from where will my help come?*
*My help comes from the LORD,*
  *who made heaven and earth.*

*(Psalm 121:1-2)*

I walked along a ridge in the northwest corner of Arkansas and couldn't remember feeling so tired or sad in a while. There was no one around as far as I could see, and I was too exhausted to be inspired.

As I walked, I realized that I was moving along a ridge right on the top of the hill. I could not lift my eyes to it because I was part of it. I was walking on the very hills that were my help to come, and I didn't see them.

Augustine of Hippo teaches that the very appearance of the created world is a great teacher of faith and theology. He tells us, "Look above you. Look below you!" The God who is our helper and the maker of heaven and earth, the God we long to be with, doesn't always speak in words or write in ink. Instead, says Augustine, "He set before your eyes the things that he has made. Can you ask for a louder voice than that?"

May we not forget today to look to the hills, even the hills we are on, to remember where our help comes from. May we remember the old prayer, that God has filled the world with beauty. May we open our eyes to behold God's gracious hand in all his works, that rejoicing in his whole creation we may learn to serve him with gladness.

God has created the earth we are walking upon; we can trust him every step of the way.

Day 3
*When the bow is in the clouds, I will see it and remember the everlasting covenant between God and every living creature of all flesh that is on the earth. (Genesis 9:16)*

I walked on a path with a great lover of nature. She taught me patiently how patterns are repeated over and over in creation, how the golden number is imprinted on everything from the cicadas to the oak leaves.

I have never been a great student of the natural world. I am just a grateful admirer of all the beauty contained within it. I admire how it points us on the spiritual path and teaches us humility.

I am not sure how anyone can walk a spiritual path without nature as one of their primary teachers. Julian of Norwich wrote, "God showed me in my palm a little thing round as a ball about the size of a hazelnut. I looked at it with the eye of my understanding and asked myself, 'What is this thing?' And I was answered. 'It is everything that is created.'"

My own journey of contemplation began with a single blade of crabgrass in my backyard. From it, I learned to make crowns of clovers and thistle paper.

When we see the wonders and mysteries of all creation in every grass and seed, in every rainbow, and in all the world's creatures, we can feel the great gift we have been given. When we see that this creation binds us to a just and loving God, we can remember the promise made to Noah that our God will never forsake us.

*Day 4*
*Give thanks in all circumstances; for this is the will of God in Christ Jesus for you.*
*(1 Thessalonians 5:18)*

Most of us want people to believe we are successful, but all of us carry our failures close to our hearts. The great news of the gospel is that in the rougher parts of the journey, our faith grows. It has been on the rougher roads that I have learned to be an advocate for people whose voice is seldom heard, and where I have experienced grace. It is why we can give thanks in all circumstances. The presence of justice does not mean the absence of failures.

When we can give thanks for everything in creation and everything in our lives, we can live the hope of Paul to the people in Thessalonica and carry the good news to everyone we see. We can see God's justice not only in the dogwoods and tulip poplars that grace our hills but also in the hackberries and ironwoods that grow at will. We can see God's mercy not only in irises and lilies that don sacred altars but also in thistles and ragweed that bless forgotten fields. We can see God's compassion for us not only in the mountain spring water that fills our glasses raised in praise but also in the waters of the Harpeth and Cumberland rivers that we have muddied. Then we can give thanks in all circumstances, not only for the successes and victories that we celebrate together, but for the brokenness and sorrow we have carried alone.

It is in the wild and unruly parts of this world that we are taught to cut new paths forward, to fight with compassion for others, to speak our truth against prevailing myths, and to humble ourselves enough to listen. If we learn these lessons and the gratitude that goes with them, we can view creation sated with thanksgiving in all circumstances, trusting that God's justice is always our companion on the journey.

*Day 5*
*Where were you when I laid the foundation*
    *of the earth?*
    *Tell me, if you have understanding.*
                        *(Job 38:4)*

I tried kicking an Osage orange down a path the other day. It just about broke my toe. Those big, green, knobby horse-apples are a mystery to me. They appear in September on the Osage orange fruit trees that mark the landscape over much of the country.

Osage oranges are able to grow in urban areas, and their thick leaves make them great for shade and protection. But their fruit litters fields and streets. If you throw one hard enough onto stone or pavement, it will break open and reveal a sticky, smelly, lime-colored substance. A walker unlucky enough to be hit on the head by a falling Osage orange could get knocked out.

As I kicked it again with the side of my foot, I wondered like a four-year-old child why in the world God created the Osage orange. Once I started pondering the mystery of the fruit, I thought of the volumes of information about creation, still unknown to me, that I long to acquire. Beyond the desire to know so that I appreciate and care for nature, does it really matter if I think a fruit is silly, or an animal beautiful, or a plant expendable? Creation is not mine to value; I am simply part of it.

I have to make peace with the idea that I will walk forever on this side of time with most of creation remaining a mystery to me. The universe is unfolding as it should, and my brief walk through it hardly gives me a sense of perspective.

In our daily walks, all of us have plenty to contemplate about the purpose of ticks, how the monarch butterfly finds its way, why the Osage orange grows, and a million deeper questions. These mysteries put us in our place alongside Job, remembering that we are part of creation, learning the meaning of it as we walk in faith. May we walk with humility in the richness of God's creation.

*Day 6*
*Whoever wants to be first must be last of all and servant of all. (Mark 9:35)*

I went on a hike with a group of about fifty people on a trail deep in the woods. Pretty soon the group was spread out, forward and back, as far as you could see. The eager, younger hikers were leading the pack; and the slower, slightly older hikers and photographers were moseying farther behind.

I was walking with the naturalist, the leader of the hike, somewhere in the back third of the group. She was explaining the unique aspects of the terrain and the flora it supported. We asked if we were slowing her down and if she needed to move to the front of the group. She replied, "You don't have to walk in front to be the leader."

The naturalist knew that leading meant serving the needs of the group wherever the need would arise. Serving meant answering our endless questions and guiding us on the path. It meant giving those who needed to be in front the opportunity, while allowing those who needed more time the freedom to saunter. She didn't need to control the walk or flaunt her knowledge before us. She was one of the finest guides I have ever met and exemplified the gospel of servant leadership without ever preaching a word.

Ralph Waldo Emerson, a great leader and teacher of nature, said that few people really know how to take a walk. He said, "What we need are more people with plain clothes, old shoes, eyes for nature, good humor, vast curiosity . . . and good silence."

May we all walk a servant's path of discipleship, even as we are called to lead. And in this manner of walking, may we never forget the guide who leads us toward peace and justice.

# Week 2. A King's Vision

*2 Samuel 23:1-4*

## Reflection

In addition to the bold claim of prophets such as Amos that the justice of God will rain down over the earth and that we will pay a price in nature for our actions toward one another, there are others in the Bible who use nature as evidence of the justice we can expect from God. One of the most powerful actors in the unfolding drama of God's justice in history is David.

David was a shepherd king who rose to power in Saul's court and united the people. He is credited with composing some of the most beautiful songs about the natural world. The Book of Second Samuel describes David's leadership on the issue of rivalries among the nomadic and agrarian tribes.

This week's reading, one of the concluding passages in that account, is a great reminder that, ultimately, rulers who fear God will allow justice to fall like rain. When leaders follow God's path, justice is as awe-inspiring and mystical as the sun rising on a cloudless morning. God's justice in creation brings us a sense of the holiness of creation. Though we may see the beauty, power, and tenderness of nature, it is but a glimpse of all that is God.

As we learn about the Israelites' understanding of God as a just God, we learn that in Hebrew, "to judge" means to be partial. In other words, God will be partial to the need for justice for the poor and will persecute and punish the oppressors. It's not the same idea as our notion of justice being blind and impartial. The early prophets, expressing the Hebrew concept, believed that justice always plays itself out in history; that justice will hold us accountable for our actions. In other words, the path of justice is important because a God of justice couldn't turn away if we hurt a neighbor or dishonored the creation or the laws of love.

In some ways, all the rhetoric and political talk about global warming continue the Hebraic understanding of God's justice. We have squandered our inheritance. We have disregarded the land and the poor. We will be held accountable unless we turn from our ways and make a right path again.

Justice is eternal and yet is capable of changing as we understand its unfolding purpose. It makes sense that in David's final speech, just before the kingship is given to Solomon, he looks back and sees how justice was always there; how it was as pervasive as rain and dew on grass. Justice was constant, even if David was not.

We can't pick a certain point on our walk and demand justice. Justice isn't carried out because we suddenly seek it or draw a line on the ground and say, "OK, now I want justice." For Israel, for David, and for us, we have broken our covenant with God to be faithful and loving to all creation. There has already been injustice, so understanding justice and becoming just is a slow process that requires our whole lives to live out.

A woman I know is going to jail for sixteen years on charges of drug possession. She has walked farther and into scarier places than I have ever been. Her walk, in fact, has been one of the most difficult I have witnessed.

She was molested as a child and was introduced to drugs at an early age. When she was picked up for possession over a year ago, the authorities released her to Magdalene, a group of residential communities for women who have criminal histories of prostitution and addiction. For a year she has been walking a path of recovery and working on her health, her job training, and her teeth.

When I met with a district attorney to discuss her case, he looked over his reading glasses at me and said, "The state demands justice, and Caesar should be paid." This is not only a misquoted phrase, but a misinterpretation of Scripture. How can justice be demanded of someone who was a victim long before she was a criminal? No one stepped in to demand justice for her; how can we demand that justice be carried out against her? And if injustice has taken root in the world, how can we ever hope for justice?

It is in times like these, when justice seems remote and unfair, that I have to believe there is a justice far greater than I can imagine. Like David, I have to learn that justice will wash over us like rain. I have to look to creation and remember that in everything I see—the rain, the sun, the grass, the trees—justice is all around me.

Over and over again in the Scriptures, we are reminded that our God is an active God. We glimpse God's actions in the work of creation, and that glimpse teaches us that the intention of our loving God is to have justice for the whole world. Sometimes, though, in the middle of the night, it is hard to believe the dawn and the dew are coming.

Robert Frost wrote that when the spirit of sorrow is with him on his walks, she loves "the bare, the withered tree." This deep sense of justice, present in all seasons, reminds us that justice permeates joy and sorrow. Justice carries us through our life and death. It is justice at work when the sap runs through trees, whether they are full or barren. We will find our peace when we trust God's justice to be active in our lives.

This week's passage from Second Samuel reminds us, through the words of David, that the existence of God is as clear as the noonday sky. We can trust God's justice because all our lives are an expression of God's actions of love. Though sometimes in the midst of the journey we might feel that the idea of injustice is stronger than justice itself, in the end we know that God always fulfills his promise to bring justice as abundantly as dew upon the grass.

It is good when we have walked long enough to trust that justice will rise like the sun, even when we are indoors with no windows to view it ourselves. We remember that truth, and we trust it.

## Questions for the Walk

1. We don't usually connect the ideas of nature and justice. What evidence of justice do you

see in the natural world? How does it affect your concept of what justice means?

2. Compare the Hebrew concept of justice with our modern, secular concept of justice. What differences do you see? Which do you think is more useful?

3. Where on your walk have you seen abundance that reminds you of justice raining down?

4. What lesson of justice can you carry back with you from today's walk?

*Walk in Silence*

## *Closing Prayer*

As a walker longs to see deer, so our souls long for justice. Gracious and merciful Lord, we pray for your justice when we see suffering in this world. Restore our troubled hearts; then remind us as we walk upon your earth that what we long for, even more than justice, is your mercy. It is by your mercy that we are given the freedom to love and serve you all the days of our lives. It is by your grace that we wake and walk this day. Amen.

# Meditations for Week 2

## Day 1

*For I command you today to love the LORD your God, to walk in his ways, and to keep his commands, decrees and laws; then you will live and increase, and the LORD your God will bless you in the land you are entering to possess. (Deuteronomy 30:16, NIV)*

St. Bernard wrote that nature is an expert that can teach us more than even the masters. He wrote that in the trees and stones we can find greater truth than we can discover in books.

Just the other day I saw that a beaver dam I cross most mornings had sprung a leak. Last summer, when the dam had been built, it had looked like one of those infinity pools as it curved perfectly around a bend in the creek. I remember thinking what a stunning feat it was for the beaver to build such a beautiful dam, chewing every one of the hardwood trees with his bare teeth. Now, looking at the washed-out dam, I felt sad, as if the old corner grocery had been torn down or the morning newspaper had gone out of business.

In hindsight I shouldn't have felt sad. The beaver chews the trees and builds the dam. The rain washes it out, and the beaver builds again. It is no more or less than justice. The beaver chews about two hundred trees a year, and part of the process is that dams break. It is just the way of the woods. It is the rhythm of life; and I need to take St. Bernard's advice, resisting the impulse to put my own meaning onto it and instead observing and learning from the master.

When we become nature's students, we adopt its laws and decrees; we are able to walk on the path and live in the land that God offers us.

*Day 2*
*This is the day that the LORD has made;*
*let us rejoice and be glad in it.*

*(Psalm 118:24)*

There is a space between darkness and sunrise. It is a dreamy time of day, marked by gray skies. The past few mornings, as I have walked at that time, the trip has been nothing less than wild. Instead of mourning doves cooing, a sound as soothing as a Buddhist bell, huge flocks of crows cluster on tree branches, shouting out high-pitched caws that set me on edge. Instead of daydreaming about the past and future, I notice the shape of the limbs, the direction of the wind, and the slight change in the crows' blackness as the sky brightens.

For me, justice in these loud woods is not found in the judgment that doves are better than crows or that I am less than either. It is in accepting the reality around us and greeting the good news of our situation with openness. Justice includes the gift of not worrying about tomorrow because we are caught up in the moment. I am not thinking about what to do; I am just doing.

Looking back on these past few mornings, I feel that the crows are reminding me to be watchful and celebrate the day. Think about all the days when we have sleepwalked through this beautiful world. The crows recall us to ourselves: to be awake and watch, to be present in the day, to be aware that this is truly the day the Lord has made. We are to rejoice and be glad in it.

The crows are a great gift on the walk of faith.

*Day 3*
    *From the depths of the grave, I called for*
      *help,*
    *and you listened to my cry.*

*You hurled me into the deep*
    *into the very heart of the seas,*
    *and the currents swirled about me. . . .*

*But you brought my life up from the pit,*
    *O LORD my God. (Jonah 2:1-6, NIV)*

In the thick of the rainforest, it's hard to see the forest for the trees. It's even harder to see the trees for the leaves. In a rainforest, everything is swirling around you; and it's hard even to read a compass to point the way out.

In some ways the experience is similar to being in the hills of Tennessee and finding that you are caught in kudzu vines or a patch of blackberry bushes. The briars catch your clothing every time you try to free yourself. In the thick of the deep wild, you can't hear yourself pray or worry about time and place. You just have to believe that however you got yourself into this mess, grace wrapped in sweet, dumb luck will be enough to get you out.

I have been lost in the darkness of a rural Ecuador night when the sound of torrential rain on a tin roof was louder than the pack of stray dogs that were barking outside the gate. As I huddled there, it was hard to remember that I was not alone; that God's justice and presence were with me in the wildest of the wild.

In the dark of moonless nights and the deep sea, you are on the other side of maps; so there is nothing to read. You can't look to rulebooks. You can't expect fairness on the path. In the fear of being abandoned where poisonous snakes make their nests, it's nothing to dream your death in a second flat.

In that space, the best tool is memory, which reminds you that you are a brother or sister of Jonah and that God will be carrying you to safety from the pit of the woods or the pit of a fish's stomach. Offer a prayer of thanksgiving, that the way out will surely be as profound as the way in.

*Day 4*
*Where you go, I will go;*
*   where you lodge, I will lodge;*
*your people shall be my people,*
*   and your God my God.*
*Where you die, I will die—*
*   there will I be buried. (Ruth 1:16b-17a)*

I want to die in the woods. It is mostly a fantasy, I know; but something about the woods makes me feel that, as mysterious as death is, the woods can sustain me.

Where the woods go, I want to go. I am Ruth, and the woods are my Naomi. When I am ready to die, I want to leave the security of indoor sanctuaries and be kissed by a fresh wind that kicks up in my presence.

I want to leave all my money and possessions without a second thought and just walk until I am tired and lie down under a sycamore, a descendant of the ones that Amos tended. I want to lie on a thick blanket of moss that I have gathered from the hillsides of my youth and cover myself in the petals of wild gardenias and lilac. I want to be near a stream on a sunny day so that the sun dances on the water and shoots color from its rays. I will close my eyes and weep at the idea of never seeing my children again, then dive into whatever it is that Ruth knew.

The woods can carry me with grace onto the other shore, of that I am sure. I am just not sure if I am graceful enough to carry out the part of Ruth.

*Day 5*
*You are the salt of the earth. But if the salt
loses its saltiness, how can it be made salty
again? (Matthew 5:13, NIV)*

Dorothy Day taught us to walk in faith with
purpose, depth, and justice. Day, cofounder of
the Catholic Worker Movement, kept a soup
kitchen operating daily for a half-century.

In her autobiography, *The Long Loneliness*,
Day emphasized that because the journey is
hard, it makes us stronger for the parts of creation that suffer. She wrote that a faith rooted
in a long walk is stronger than anything, even
death, and that spreading the kingdom of God
upon the earth is more sublime and compelling
than anything we have yet to comprehend.

Dorothy Day was the salt of the earth; and
the saltiness came from her courage and humble faith, her defiance and surrender. She spiced
the pot so the rest of us could taste those gifts.
Through trials and suffering, her faith never
lost its usefulness or beauty. Her life was
a statement calling us to surrender to the truth of

God and to remember that there are far greater thoughts than anything we have thought so far.

Salt, because of its importance in ancient times, was mentioned more than forty times in the Bible. Salt deposits were formed in the evaporation of ancient salt lakes. Salt was harvested and used to preserve things that people wanted to hold on to. To be the salt of the earth, therefore, means that we are connected to ancient waters; that we preserve justice and hold on to the faith that has been handed down to us.

It is a good thing to be salt. It means we come from the earth and carry the earth on every step of our walk.

*Day 6*
*Deep calls to deep*
  *at the thunder of your cataracts.*
                                    *(Psalm 42:7a)*

Deep truths in the caverns of the earth are there for us to behold, but we cannot attain them without being in communion with the earth itself. Deep calls to deep, but we can't hear it if we don't scratch below the surface to see what flows beneath.

When we take time to go to the deepest places in our hearts, we find the miraculous nature of God's handiwork written not only on the walls of caverns, but on the backside of leaves and the underside of moss. In all the secrets of the world, the beauty of God's truth is almost too much to behold.

Walt Whitman wrote in "Song of Myself" that he once went to a place of creation so profound, he could see that "a leaf of grass is no less than the journey work of the stars. And the pleasure is equally perfect." When we are graced to walk in such a place, we realize how rich our lives are—full of miracles as common as a mockingbird, as magical as a maple leaf, as abundant as an acorn on a fall morning in the hills of Tennessee.

We long for deep places on our walks. They connect us to God and keep us centered.

# Week 3. A Personal Vision

*Job 12:7-13*

## Reflection

In this series I quote Job as much as any other book of the Bible. It is a dramatic and compelling story about God's justice and how it relates to the state of creation. The story of Job is a great follow-up to the visions of justice given to us by Amos and David.

If you remove the prologue and epilogue of Job, which many scholars think were added later, you are left with a profound and poetic dialogue about a man who perseveres despite the apparent lack of justice in his life. The book deals with one of the most basic and fundamental questions of faith: What does it mean for the innocent to suffer? In the unfolding story, Job's three friends, who think they are defending God, challenge Job; but he always argues with them and finally is allowed to speak to God about the injustice of life.

Some of the beliefs that are challenged in the Book of Job include the idea that God is just and that God is the source of justice. Amos and David, who supported those beliefs, lived in the pre-exilic world of Israel; so they were addressing people who were oppressed and for whom justice meant liberation.

For Amos and David, justice was experienced in events such as the Exodus and in people such as the judges, who were seen as heroes to those suffering. God's justice meant that people would have land and enough to eat; it was a saving justice. If the faithful who had been the recipients of such justice didn't act faithfully, they would receive the other side of justice; and there would be destruction.

But Job is writing after the Israelites have returned from exile, when they have lost their possessions and are rebuilding. They are trying to understand justice in a new light. Job reminds the people, and us, that it is hard to square our real-life experiences with what ought to be or what we think we deserve. He asks us to consider a difficult question: What does justice mean in a human life that has seen no justice?

The answer for Job is filled with layers of meaning. Job learns that the faithful and wise servant who doesn't settle for easy answers is the person who gets to wrestle with God on the path of justice. Job's difficult questions about justice are not answered; instead, he accepts that as part of creation he is subject to a justice far greater than he, or we, can comprehend. The justice he confronts is not our justice; and thus we, along with Job, must learn humility. As we trace the unfolding story, we learn that justice must include mystery and compassion.

To arrive at this new and more difficult understanding of justice, Job looks to animals, birds, and plants. He remembers that their lives, like his, come from the Creator; and the way to gain wisdom is not just by living, but by contemplating the creation all around us.

In the story of Job, justice is shown to be more than reward or retribution; it is surrender to the creator of life itself and trust in his wisdom. In that surrender, we behold the gift of creation;

and by observing and embracing it, we learn more about the attributes of the One who created it all. When Job's friends ask questions about justice, he tells them to look around and learn more about the creation.

Maybe we all should try to be naturalists. A naturalist is not necessarily a scientist, but a person who goes into nature, observes, and takes notes. This way of seeing ourselves has implications for how we study Scripture. Scripture, filled with naturalists' notes about the creation, offers clues about our creator.

We return to nature again and again, in much the same way that we keep going back to Scripture. Both are the living word of God, bringing us life and light. Both teach us about a creator whose peace, justice, and love are unfolding before us.

In my twenty years of ministry, most of the visions I have had for living an ideal of justice were born in the quiet of the woods. Every program I have helped to start was begun, in part, from contemplation with God in the woods. In that solitude I have found a safe place to wrestle with the injustices of the world.

Over the years I have discovered that the more I contemplate and wrestle with issues of justice in the woods, the better at contemplation and wrestling I become. Job is a great model for both. He is not satisfied with easy answers or the assurances of faithful people around him. He goes to creation and asks God for himself, Why is the world so unfair? By going directly to God with the question, Job finds a deeper path within; and so can we.

When I started the Magdalene community, a group that serves women coming out of jail and off the streets who have criminal histories of prostitution, violence, and addiction, I walked for days in the woods, wondering if I really believed that mercy could be as powerful a teacher as justice. What I contemplated was in some ways small and simple. I envisioned a single house outside judicial systems and religious authority. It would be free of charge and would welcome women without judgment. It would be a sanctuary for healing. It would be a place with no set authority, where women could wrestle with some of the hard questions and stay in community. Those thoughts were not new or unique; they go back as far as Job. What was special was that in the woods, that old vision was given space to germinate and grow in my heart. Fifteen years later, we have six communities and over one hundred women who have graduated from the two-year program.

Sometimes when I walk long enough and far enough, I can feel hope rising in me from the justice and peace that abide in the woods. All the anger I have felt about injustice inspires me to work harder. All the frustration I have felt about my own complacency and ignorance dissipates into a deep gratitude that I still have the will to serve others.

In the woods, all of us, like Job, are free enough to tap into the anger we carry with us and to demand answers from the source of life. In the woods, ideas are not judged; instead, they are given room to grow, to take root, and to blossom into something beautiful.

Since there is no judgment in the woods, we are not bound by preconceived myths. We are not forced to stay in a box; there really aren't any boxes in the woods. We get to sort through

things, dream new things, and pray that we have
the will to carry out the lessons of the woods.

### Questions for the Walk

1. Which bird, animal, or plant teaches you
   something about the divine nature of justice? What does it teach?

2. Compare the concepts of justice presented
   by Amos and David with those in the Book
   of Job. What are the differences, and which
   do you think is more valid?

3. "Maybe we should all try to be naturalists."
   If you tried to be a naturalist in your life
   and your study of Scripture, what things
   might you do?

4. When you go into nature, what do you
   learn; and how do you learn it?

### Walk in Silence

## *Closing Prayer*

Give us wise and compassionate hearts, to care for your decrees, to love your creation, and to wrestle with hard truths in deep conversation. Show us your mercy on our walk, and help us to stand without judgment of one another. Give us good companions on the walk, and bring us safely to our journey's end. All for love's sake. Amen.

# *Meditations for Week 3*

*Day 1*
*Let us not become weary in doing good, for*
*at the proper time we will reap a harvest if*
*we do not give up. (Galatians 6:9, NIV)*

There isn't any reason to tire of walking on
a regular basis. Sometimes we may need to take
a break from our routine; but if we stop the
practice of walking entirely, we will soon forget
the lessons we have learned.

Walking is a religious discipline, like prayer,
that needs to be practiced over and over and
over. There isn't a point in our prayer life when
we think we are done praying, as if there won't
be a new prayer in the next breath. The same is
true of walking. There can't be a day when we
stop walking the path of faith, or loving our
neighbors, or doing good. None of these things
are on a "to do" list; they are just part of our
daily pilgrimage.

The place where I can most easily walk and not grow tired is in the hills of Maine on summer mornings. You can walk for miles and miles and never grow weary because wild blueberries grow all along the path, offering refreshment every step of the way.

Wild blueberries are reminders that grace is free. It's fun to take off a ball cap and fill it up with blueberries when you pass by and dream of all the people you want to share them with when you return, your belly full and your lips stained dark from the juice.

Blueberries are a living example of Paul's lessons to the Galatians. We don't get tired of being the church or of walking or of doing good because grace comes our way and offers us a harvest when we need it.

*Day 2*
*Do you believe because I told you that I saw you under the fig tree? You will see greater things than these. (John 1:50)*

It's hard to imagine anything greater than the Lord recognizing us under the fig tree. To be known is just about the best feeling in the world. To be remembered when standing under an old fig tree where a million other hikers have stood is unbelievable.

There is a line of big, old fig trees on a beautiful avenue in Nashville. The fig trees are indigenous to western Asia but were brought into the Mediterranean landscape over five thousand years ago. They are beautiful trees that grow up to thirty feet tall. Their branches are muscular and twisting, spreading wider than they are tall. I love walking under those trees and remembering that Nathanael was standing under their cousin when Jesus walked by and remembered him.

I think sometimes that if we stand under the fig tree and remember that all of us are part of the trees and plants and land and seas, we will see greater things, as the Gospel of John promises. We see the intricate web of veins in every leaf of the tree. We see figs that have fallen at our feet, containing seeds to grow more trees.

We see the twisted bark that stretches out to animals and birds as a welcome home.

In that one fig tree we see the whole universe unfolding as it should. We are standing under it; and somewhere in the universe that we call the mind of God, we have been remembered.

*Day 3*
*Stand still, and consider the wondrous works of God. (Job 37:14, KJV)*

Once in Ecuador we drove up to a high mountain called Corazon, which means "the heart." A group of us were on our third pilgrimage to a small school, and after several days of activity we couldn't figure out how to move our project forward. So some of us got together with the teachers, climbed into a van, and took a day off.

We went to the mountain, hoping for a sign or some idea of what we should do. We spent hours in the van climbing slowly toward the peak, then got out and trekked the rest of the way on foot, over steep stones on dramatic cultivated hillsides where Ecuadorian farmers seemed to live diagonally. We climbed into the clouds, where the drizzle sat on our skin and we couldn't see the person ahead or behind. We knew we were at the top when there was nowhere left to climb.

Standing at the edge of the mountain, I saw only dense, gray, cold fog. I heard scattered voices talking and laughing about being soaked and cold. I stood still and closed my eyes. Then, maybe because of all the climbing, or my desire to be with God, or the moisture acting like a prism in the thin mountain air, I saw the colors of a rainbow, like ripples in a pond, dancing before my eyes. I think those dancing circles of color behind my eyes on Corazon may be as close as I ever come to seeing the wonders and mysteries of God.

Then someone called out that it was time to go back to the school and work.

*Day 4*
*He calls for the waters of the sea*
*And pours them out on the face of the earth;*
*The LORD is his name. (Amos 5:8c, NKJV)*

Standing on the edge of the ocean, I can feel the moon pulling the tide that is pulling me closer to heaven.

There is not a better place to see the spiritual nature of the world than on the shore. Looking out over the ocean is about as close as we get to imagining infinity. The sound of the waves fills our ears and sets our hearts in a slow, steady rhythm.

I walked on a beautiful shore, and my tears tasted the same as the water splashing around my legs. We are made of the same salty water that flows over the earth. Whenever I cry or work hard enough to sweat, I am part of Amos' vision of the ocean pouring out onto the earth. My salt, as well as the ocean's, flows easily onto the ground. When it returns to the earth, I become part of the work of justice pouring out onto the land. Salty waters are the deepest and are called by God out of this ocean in a million ways to find their way onto the earth.

I am a drop in the ocean. I can walk this path in reverence for the sea and the Holy One

who calls the waters to move. It moves in
waves; and when we stand in their path with
proper reverence, we can offer our drop
with gratitude for the creator of this water.

*Day 5*
*Teach me, O LORD, the way of thy statutes;*
   *and I shall keep it unto the end.*
                              *(Psalm 119:33, KJV)*

It's hard to unlearn things.

Recently I had to unlearn that bears hiber-
nate. I found out that instead of hibernating,
they are in fact "denning," meaning that the
bear's body temperature remains relatively sta-
ble and the bear can be easily aroused. Once
my understanding of what the bear does in
winter had changed, the way I thought about
the bear and even my language had to change
along with it.

Then I had to unlearn that Pluto is a planet.
Instead, it's the largest member of the Kuiper
belt and a "dwarf planet." I had carried in my
head an image of the nine planets circling the

sun, based on painted polystyrene balls suspended on wire. I had to discard that image before I could take in the idea that Pluto is one of a group of small, icy objects beyond Neptune that are similar in orbit, size, and composition.

The art of learning God's decrees may begin with unlearning things and then learning again by simple observation of the natural world. We should walk as students, ready to unlearn and take notes, grateful for any new pieces of information that come our way. In this way, when we learn a new statute, it will be easy to take it to heart, to follow it all the days of our lives, and to share it with other pilgrims.

*Day 6*
*The LORD told Moses, "Go up into the Abarim Range. . . . There on the mountain that you have climbed you will die. . . . You will see the land only from a distance."*
*(Deuteronomy 32:48-52, NIV)*

Moses, giver of the law, spent forty years in the desert leading people toward the Promised Land.

In his travels he climbed Mount Sinai, dreaming of the day when he could stop wandering.

Toward the end of his life, Moses was called by God to the mountain one last time. There Moses saw the Promised Land, his heart's desire; but God told Moses that he would die before crossing the Jordan. Moses lay down and died as God commanded. He never was able to see the benefits of faithfully wandering and leading the people.

It is a powerful image: Moses the leader, dying in the desert. The image is a testimony to his obedience and love of God. It is a reminder of how powerless we are over where we are headed. Yet, even though Moses never reached the Promised Land, his law crossed into Jerusalem and is the law we write on our children's hearts.

The story of Moses teaches us to trust that nothing beloved by God is ever lost, even though life seems unfair and sometimes we struggle to obey the laws of faith. God's acts of love live beyond our temporal lives. Moses must have held a glimpse of the great law of love that is eternal.

# Week 4. Jesus' Vision

*Luke 13:6-9*

## Reflection

This parable of the barren fig tree begins as a harsh statement about justice. It is a warning to the community of faith that a barren tree, unless it brings forth fruit, will be cut down. This parable refers to the nation and its faithless institutions and leaders that are more worried about their power than about justice.

The parable also serves as an awakening to all communities of faith, that we are experiencing a season of grace that we should not take for granted. None of us is doing all we can do to usher in the kingdom of God, so we should feel grateful that we have been given another season to live more faithfully and love one another more fully. We should use the season to produce the fruits of faith. We should remember that this is the season to prune and dig and offer justice in more tangible and visible ways to those who are in need.

God has borne our fruitless faith for many seasons, the parable reminds us. Our hope lies in our God, who will bear us a little longer. In Luke's Gospel, Jesus is portrayed as the Great Physician; and he offers a ministry of compassion that seeks to include everyone. He seeks out the lost and binds up the wounded. He criticizes only those who have power and authority; anyone who needs help or is suffering is given comfort. When viewed in that light, this week's passage sounds less like a threat and more like an invitation.

The problems that Jesus encounters in Luke stem from the religious and political leaders who feel threatened by his radical message of love without judgment. If the church or the authorities try to stop growth, they should be cut down because they are not producing the fruits of faith. This parable exemplifies the idea of justice without judgment. On the one hand, it is a parable of compassion, providing comfort for the disciple who stumbles along the way. On the other hand, it is a parable about crisis that should light a fire under those who think they have power and authority and don't have to work toward ushering in the kingdom of God.

For a naturalist, nothing compares to the beauty of a tree heavy-laden with fruit. Last year four of us walked through a plant nursery in the coastal region of Ecuador. We wanted to buy herbs to plant at a nearby school. After looking at some herbs, we noticed a small gate hidden at the back of the nursery. When we stepped through the gate, we found a beautiful arbored path stretched out before us, flanked by a vast orchard of terraced hillsides filled with mango and cocoa fruits.

It was beautiful standing there just before the harvest. This must have been the vision that Jesus had in mind when he spoke about the fruit tree. There is nothing more hopeful than walking through an orchard in fruit-bearing season. The trees were created for this very task, and they have become exactly what they were meant to be. They are the living embodiment of a plentiful harvest. There is prosperity and life in the branches that have been tended, pruned, and given the time and space to blossom into this magnificent sight.

This parable, like many of the parables, is a reminder that we all need to repent on the path of justice. None of us has truly carried our weight or borne the fruit we are capable of producing. The task Jesus sets before us is not really so hard. Fruit trees must bear fruit. They need freedom and tender care. Jesus is telling us that, though he is compassionate, he won't let faith be misused. Nowhere in the Gospels does he use vengeance or harbor anger in pursuing the ideals of justice, but in his own firm way he upholds justice for the sake of the Kingdom.

Jesus calls for the trees to bear fruit, and he calls us to live the life for which we were created. All of us can bear fruit. All of us can go to the mountaintop like the prophets and have visions of justice and glimpses of God. It seems unbelievable, but we all carry that ability within us. One tiny dream of justice rising in our hearts is enough to carry us there, on just a whisper of a prayer. The community of Luke—and before that, the commnity of Amos and Moses—passed down the map to the mountain so we could dream of justice and bear good fruit.

A tree that can bear fruit, like a faith that can bear justice, is living out its purpose. As long as there is hope for a harvest, we should keep working toward that end. But if there is no hope for justice and no desire to bear good fruit, our trees should fall to make room for new trees that will thrive and help to bring about God's kingdom.

## *Questions for the Walk*

1. What fruits do you feel you are bearing in your life? Do you think they are fruits you are well-suited to bear?

2. What fruits could you be bearing that you are not currently bearing? What might you do to start bearing those fruits?

3. Have you had a mountaintop experience in which you felt that you had glimpsed God? Describe the experience and how you responded.

*Walk in Silence*

*Closing Prayer*
*(from the* Book of Common Prayer*)*

Almighty and everlasting God, you made the universe with all its marvelous order, its atoms, worlds, and galaxies, and the infinite complexity of living creatures: Grant that, as we probe the mysteries of your creation, we may come to know you more truly, and more surely fulfill our role in your eternal purpose. In giving us dominion over things on earth, you made us fellow workers in your creation: Give us wisdom and reverence so to use the resources of nature, that no one may suffer from our abuse of them, and that generations yet to come may continue to praise you for your bounty; through Jesus Christ our Lord. Amen.

# Meditations for Week 4

## Day 1

*Lead me in the path of your commandments, for I delight in it. (Psalm 119:35)*

There are strict rules in nature. The grace is that in complete surrender to those rules, nature becomes absolutely free.

I would love to be that free. If I could quit worrying so much about balance and strive instead to surrender to the eternal laws of love, I think I would be a lot freer.

The laws of love, written in Deuteronomy, were used by the psalmists and summarized by Jesus when he said, "You shall love the Lord your God with all your heart, and with all your soul, and with all your strength, and with all your mind; and your neighbor as yourself" (Luke 10:27).

When we surrender everything to that law, we will saunter in delight, like the psalmist.

Yesterday on a walk, I saw a pileated woodpecker. He was singing to beat the band and flying around the trees, banging his red head into the bark to find his next meal. The woodpecker was just doing what woodpeckers do, but it was a delight to watch him and see him sing and dance in the trees. It is not something the woodpecker strives to do; it is the way he is.

We are led to follow the commandments of God, not to be burdened, but to be released. We will be as free as the wild animals, moving easily down the path set before us. It is not our obligation; it is our delight.

*Day 2*
*And Moses said, "When the LORD gives you meat to eat in the evening and your fill of bread in the morning, because the LORD has heard the complaining that you utter against him—what are we? Your complaining is not against us but against the LORD."*

*(Exodus 16:8)*

There is a difference between imagining that you are wandering in the desert and actually wandering in the desert.

I remember entering the dunes in Namibia as a visitor eager to take in the vistas. I climbed up and down for hours with a cold, gritty wind against my cheeks, at a height that caught my breath because of the danger of falling. Struggling to keep my footing, I made inchworm progress. I tried to keep my family in sight, while at the same time staying near to the young Namibian guide who was being so patient with me.

That landscape was different from the bushes and gentle features of the Kalahari Desert through which I had hiked previously. This was the harshest environment I had experienced, and I wondered how it would be possible to live there. I couldn't imagine it.

When you're at home, sitting on the patio or standing at a sink that has running water, it's easy to imagine what a desert trip might be like. You would pack camels with thick blankets; and as you reached a spot near the coast, you would pitch a big tent, watch the magnificent sunset, and spend the evening enjoying a feast. But when I was hiking there, tasting dust no matter how much water I drank, I just wanted to find shelter, eat something, and rest.

Sometimes I think we are so far removed from the environments of Scripture that we think it would be easy to do things differently. We wouldn't need to murmur in the desert and complain against God; we would have complete faith in Moses. But when I remember my single day in a Namibian desert, I sympathize with the wandering Israelites.

Their story is a reminder of how important leadership is and how easily we can get lost. It is a reminder that justice can feel foreign when you are oppressed by your environment. It makes me profoundly grateful for a forgiving God who kept feeding and loving the people.

*Day 3*
*The angel of the LORD found Hagar near*
*a spring in the desert. . . . And he said,*

*"Hagar, servant of Sarai, where have you come from, and where are you going?"*
*(Genesis 16:7-8a, NIV)*

I was walking in the North Carolina woods when an old crow sitting in a branch sang a strange new song. It had more notes than I was used to and sounded almost backward. It startled me and brought me out of a daydream into the power and presence of the woods where I was walking.

The crow is known as a harbinger of truth, so to hear him sing a new song made me think about new truths and the way old ideas must sometimes shift to make room for new ones— the way a pregnant woman's organs must shift to make room for the new baby.

There are many ideas in the world, and only a few sink in through our thick skin. A smaller number find their way deep into our minds, and only one in a million goes further still and takes up residence in our hearts. That is the place that influences our actions and moves us to act in faith without fear.

The old crow was like a descendant of the angel who met Hagar in the desert. That crow brought me a new truth and helped me remember that sometimes we need to be tested to expand our understanding of truth and justice. Every now and then, in the deep woods of our lives, we need the crow to ask us, "Where have you come from, and where are you going?"

*Day 4*
*He appointed the moon for seasons;*
*    The sun knows its going down.*
*                              (Psalm 104:19, NKJV)*

Francis of Assisi wrote that there is no use in walking anywhere to preach unless our walking is our preaching. That is a perfect way, it seems to me, to think about walking the path of justice.

If we want to walk the path of justice, we have to celebrate the goodness of the night and the day. We have to know that the moon and the sun work together to make a season and that all seasons come and go until the circle comes around and we begin all over again. We live out justice in every step we take so that by the time we get back home, justice will be with us.

There is justice in the cover of darkness as well as in the light; it's just harder to see it, as the psalmist reminds us. There is a season to harvest under a full moon. There is a different season to plant new blossoms under another full moon so that the next crop can grow. Both seasons are steps in the cycle of growing, and both are important to the fulfillment of justice.

The rhythm of justice surely is found in our steps upon this earth. Justice falls on the heels of the peace we make with all the seasons of our journey. We must make peace with life and death, with the sun and moon, with our comings and goings, so we don't lose track of the path of justice we travel.

Justice will keep us walking in the right direction and be our companion along the way, even as we search for it.

*Day 5*
*I will give you shepherds after my own heart,*
*who will feed you with knowledge and*
*understanding. (Jeremiah 3:15)*

We can't judge anyone else's walk until we
know how to walk perfectly, and all of us have
a long way to go.

Pierre-Auguste Renoir, at the age of seventy-
two, said he was just learning how to paint. In
his sixties, Renoir began to suffer from rheuma-
tism, which eventually crippled him and con-
fined him to a wheelchair; even so, he continued
to paint until the end of his life in 1919. In his
last years he was unable to move his hands; but
he still painted, using a brush his assistants
would strap to his arm. It was a remarkable
witness to humility by a master artist. He never
thought he had perfected the skill of painting;
he simply felt that the artist's job was to keep
painting until he couldn't paint anymore.

Henry David Thoreau maintained that it
takes an entire life to learn how to walk well.
Thoreau said he had only met a few people

who understood walking and had a genius for it. "Sauntering" was the term he used to describe the way people walk when they feel as if they are at home wherever they go. Such people head out on a walk and feel that they never have to return; it is a walk that lasts a lifetime.

The prophet Jeremiah knew the depths of despair, had witnessed the destruction of his home, and still believed in the greatness of God's love. He kept prophesying, never thinking he had arrived, but instead believing there was always more to do for the sake of love. His last recorded words were uttered during exile in Egypt; and they call us to walk faithfully, always seeing the work ahead as a gift.

Masters such as Renoir, Thoreau, and Jeremiah understand that we cannot attain perfection in our art until we are done living it. Until then, we should withhold judgment of others, who after all, like us, are works in progress.

*Day 6*
*When Jesus realized that they were about to come and take him by force to make him*

*king, he withdrew again to the mountain by himself. (John 6:15)*

What saves me from cynicism about the institutional church is gratitude. What cultivates gratitude is getting away from the people and places that have a claim on me and walking in the woods. In the woods I begin to sense something between God and me that feels like genuine prayer.

We need solitude so justice has room to breathe. Solitude is very different from loneliness. It is the place where our internal sense of the world gets in step with the way we walk in the world.

In the woods we have time and space to reflect on life; in that reflection, it is easier to see grace and mercy. We just have to start walking, and the feelings seem to rise up. From nowhere, gratitude and lightness begin to grow in our hearts.

As we walk alone and pray, we may not find justice; yet we can rest assured that we are closer to its source. Julian of Norwich, a mystic in the 1300s, wrote, "I was taught in my mind that seeking is as good as seeing." We seek with grateful hearts, hearts full of gratitude for the gift of nature and the ways it manifests the nature of God.

When I am able to walk for a whole morning, I feel that my spirit has been reconnected to God. I am ready to go back from the secret place and seek justice in the public spaces again.

# The Sacred Ground of Burning Bushes

It could have been the sun
Blushing from kissing the day goodbye,
Or the reflection off a creek on a late afternoon.
It could have been an early redbud blooming,
Startled awake by the beauty of the passing day,
Or a field of fire-pink rising from the ashes of winter.
It called me as deep calls to deep.

I followed it deep into the hollow of my woods,
Fear and liberation walking down the aisle toward life.
Bound for seasons, bare feet walked
on a wet, cold ground.
In the whitest flames I was consumed,
And felt a Pentecostal crown set upon my head.
In dancing shadows I felt the pain of poverty
And the burden of riches that feel like death.

I heard nothing but God's voice rising,
Not just from the flame, but the woods itself.
My face, hot to the touch,
was soothed by salty gratitude.

The smell of lavender, olive, and geranium
Rose like incense uncontained on upward drafts.
It melted my heart as easily as iron in the kiln,
My heart fashioning itself to love.

Turning away with an aftertaste burning my heart,
I grieved this specter may never light this ground again,
But pray its light carries me
through interminable nights,
Unforgiving waters and undue seasons.
Putting my shoes back on my beloved feet,
I turn from myself so that this fresh heart of flesh
Can grow and flower in its transfigured grace.

# *Notes*

Page 31, Augustine. See http://vaumc.org/NCFile
Repository/ChurchSociety/CreationCareResources.
pdf. (5-25-10)

Page 33, Julian of Norwich. See http://www.sps.edu/
common/news_detail.asp?newsid=436860&L1=&L
2=&tabs=news. (5-25-10)

Page 39, Emerson. See http://www.quotationsbook.com/
quote/13182/. (5-25-10)

Page 45, Frost. See http://www.brainyquote.com/
quotes/quotes/r/robertfros151806.html. (5-25-10)

Page 58, Whitman. See http://www.tropicsoft.com/
EdwardDiener/Literature/whitman.html. (5-25-10)

Page 82, Closing Prayer. Taken from "For Knowledge
of God's Creation" and "For the Conservation of
Natural Resources," in the Book of Common
Prayer, American Edition (Oxford University Press,
1979); page 827. See also http://ww.bcponline.org.

Page 88, Francis of Assisi. See http://creative
quotations.com/one/2393.htm. (6-2-10)

Pages 90–91, Thoreau. See http://www.vcu.edu/
engweb/transcendentalism/authors/thoreau/
walking/. (6-2-10)

Pages 92–93, Julian of Norwich. See http://www.
gloriana.nu/showings.htm. (5-25-10)